one of us
HORSES

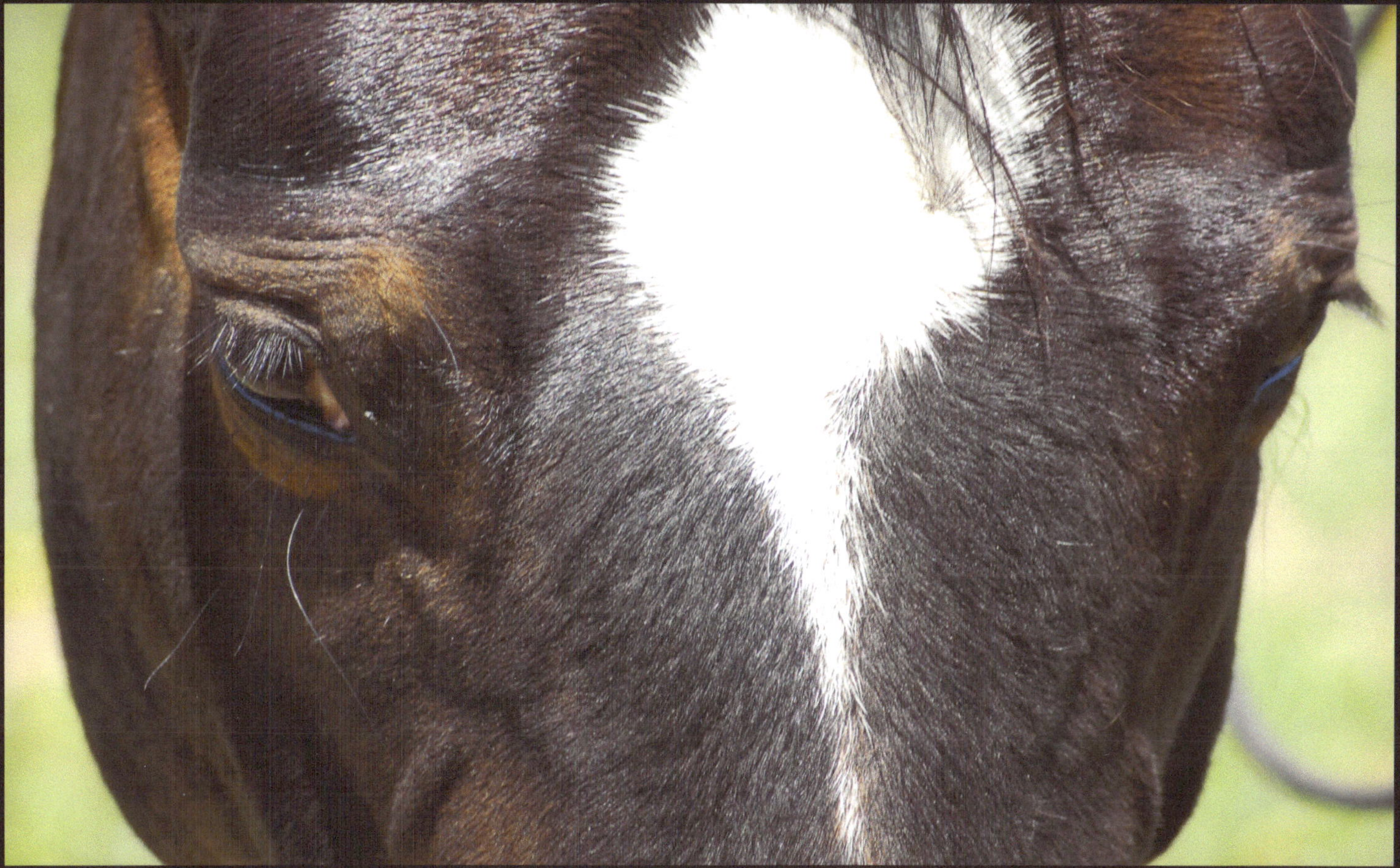

F O R W A R D

Elizabeth Tanner's horses wlecome you into their midst as if you were one of the herd.

I have the privilidge of working with horses everyday. They reveal their likes, dislikes,

friendships and interests through their gestures, antics and attitudes.

Beth captures their individualities as they do what comes naturally out in the pasture.

So-leave their bridles behind for today and just enjoy their company, in their world.

-Iris Moore, 20112

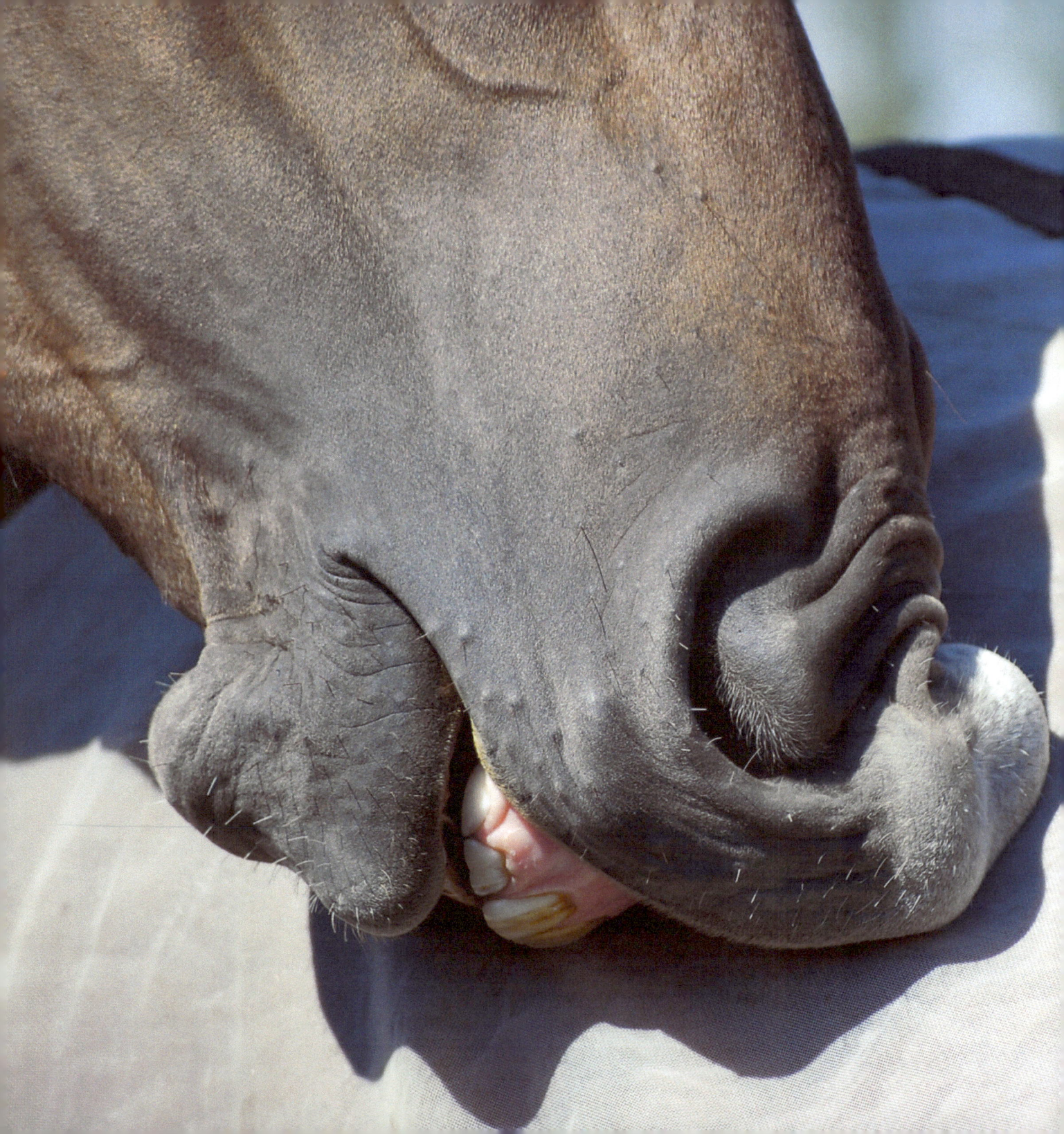

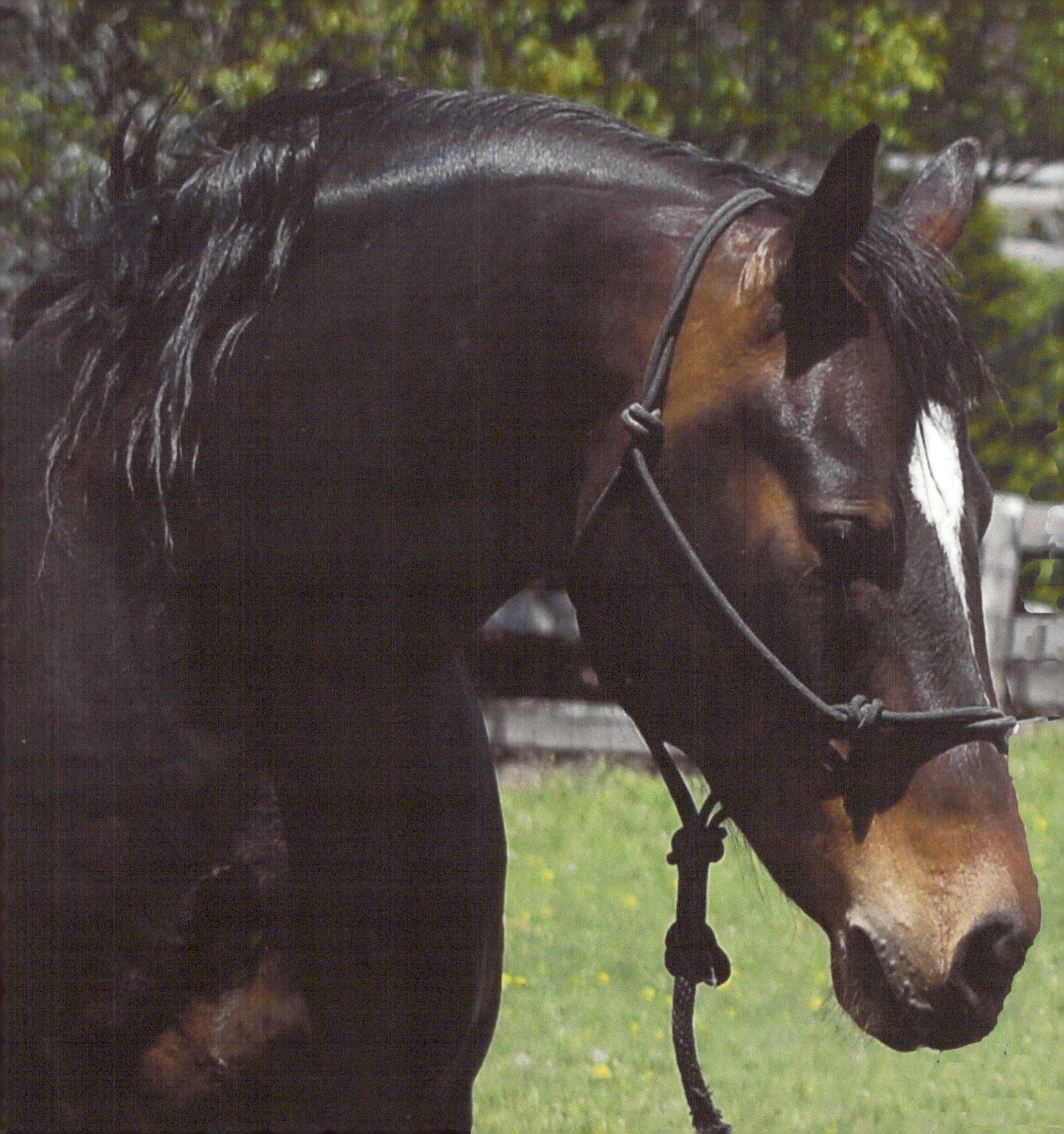

Thanks to everyone who let me spend time with their
animals, and to the animals themselves.
It was an unforgettable experience.
Elizabeth Tanner